Cool
OUTDOOR
ARTS & CRAFTS

Great Things to Do in the Great Outdoors

Alex Kuskowski

**Checkerboard
Library**

An Imprint of Abdo Publishing
abdopublishing.com

abdopublishing.com

Published by Abdo Publishing, a division of ABDO,
PO Box 398166, Minneapolis, Minnesota 55439.
Copyright © 2016 by Abdo Consulting Group, Inc.
International copyrights reserved in all countries. No
part of this book may be reproduced in any form without
written permission from the publisher. Checkerboard
Library™ is a trademark and logo of Abdo Publishing.

Printed in the United States of America,
North Mankato, Minnesota
062015
092015

Content Developer: Nancy Tuminelly
Design and Production: Jen Schoeller, Mighty Media, Inc.
Series Editor: Liz Salzmann
Photo Credits: Frankie and Maclean Potts, Jen Schoeller,
Shutterstock

The following manufacturers/names appearing in this
book are trademarks: 3M™, 3M™ Scotch®, Craft Smart®,
Duck Tape®, Gorilla Glue™, Krylon® ColorMaster™, Loew
Cornell®, Mod Podge®, Morton®, Rust-oleum® Painter's
Touch®, Sharpie®, Thompson's® WaterSeal®, Tulip® Soft
Fabric Paint™, VersaColor™

Library of Congress Cataloging-in-Publication Data
Kuskowski, Alex.
  Cool outdoor arts & crafts : great things to do in the
great outdoors / Alex Kuskowski.
     pages cm. -- (Cool great outdoors)
  Audience: Grade 3 to 6.
  Includes index.
   ISBN 978-1-62403-697-2
1. Handicraft--Juvenile literature. 2. Nature craft--
Juvenile literature. 3. Outdoor recreation--Juvenile
literature. I. Title. II. Title: Cool outdoor arts and crafts.
  TT160.K872 2016
  745.5--dc23
                          2014045316

To Adult Helpers:

This is your chance to inspire kids to
get outside! As children complete the
activities in this book, they'll develop new
skills and confidence. They'll even learn
to love and appreciate the great outdoors!

Some of the activities in this book will
require your help, but encourage kids to
do as much as they can on their own. Be
there to offer guidance when needed, but
mostly be a cheerleader for their creative
spirit and natural inspirations!

Before getting started, it helps to review
the activities and set some ground
rules. Remind kids that cleaning up is
mandatory! Adult supervision is always
recommended. So is going outside!

CONTENTS

Get Crafty!

Do you like arts and crafts? Do you like to paint? Do you like to glue things together? Do you like to make decorations? The outdoors can be a great inspiration for your creativity!

We spend most of our lives inside. Take a second to count the hours. You sleep inside. You eat inside. You study inside. That's life in the 21st century.

You've got to get out!

You can make projects that bring nature indoors. You can make projects to decorate the outdoors! It all happens outside. And it's all good. They don't call it the great outdoors for nothing!

A NATURAL RECHARGE!

What's so great about the great outdoors? A lot! Being outside exposes us to the sun's natural light. The sun gives us **vitamin** D. Vitamin D keeps our bodies strong! Exposure to sunlight helps regulate our sleeping patterns. The more you are outside, the easier it is to fall asleep!

NATURE *Is the Original* MUSE

Artistic inspiration can come from anywhere. The natural world has inspired artists throughout history. A tree, a river, or even a breeze can be a **muse**.

Think of the art in your home or school. Have you ever seen a photograph of a sunset? Or a painting of a sailboat on the water? These are examples of art coming from nature. When we go outside, we are often inspired!

Bringing Together the
OUTDOORS & ART

How can you use the great outdoors in your artwork? Any way you want! Take a look below for inspiration!

Using Natural Materials

Some artists use natural materials to create art.

Preserving Nature

Some artists preserve nature in its original form.

Did You Know?

Pineapples are a symbol of **hospitality**. That's why they are often carved or painted near entryways.

Seeing Nature in Your Own Way

Art doesn't have to look exactly like the nature it imitates.

Literal Translations

Some artists want their art to really look like it does in nature!

Art Goes
INSIDE & OUT

*D*oes art belong inside or outside? The answer is both! The art projects in this book are all about the outdoors. Some of the art is for display indoors. Some of it you'll even wear!

ARE YOU READY?

1. Check the Weather
Check the forecast before you begin any outdoor adventure!

2. Dress Appropriately
Dress in layers! Be prepared for a **variety** of temperatures.

3. Bring Water
It's important to drink enough water, especially if it's hot out.

4. Get Permission
Some of the activities in this book require adult **supervision**. When in doubt, ask for help!

Bringing the Outdoors In
Ever notice how houseplants change a room? There's something really cool about bringing the outdoors inside!

Bringing the Indoors Out
Bling up your backyard, porch, **balcony**, or deck with your art! There's no reason to keep art indoors!

Now let's get out and enjoy the great outdoors!

Materials

Here are some of the things you'll need.

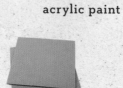

acrylic paint

beads

black duct tape

blue painter's tape

cardboard

clear tape

coarse sea salt

drawer knobs

fabric paint

flexible rubber stamps

foam brush

food coloring

googly eyes

Gorilla Glue

ink pad

leaf

LED tea lights

mason jars

measuring spoons

Mod Podge

newspaper

paintbrush

paper plates

permanent
marker

plant stake

plastic
container

plastic wrap

plastic yard
flamingo

puffy paint

rocks

ruler

scissors

spray paint

spray sealer

terra-cotta pot

toothpicks

twine

white cotton
scarf

ROCK ON!

Materials

newspaper
smooth rocks
flexible rubber stamps
ink pad
spray sealer
acrylic paint
paintbrush

Stamped Rocks

1. Find **flexible** stamps that fit on the rocks. Cover your work surface with newspaper.

2. Press a stamp onto the ink pad. Make sure the ink gets on the details of the stamp.

3. Remove the stamp from the ink pad. Be careful to only touch the dry side.

4. Place the stamp ink side down on a rock. Press firmly. Press the edges down on any curves. Lift the stamp off.

5. Repeat steps 2 through 4 to stamp more rocks. Let the ink dry.

6. Place the stamped rocks on newspaper. Coat them with spray sealer. Let them dry.

Painted Rocks

1 Find unusually shaped rocks. Cover your work surface with newspaper.

2 Paint the rocks with acrylic paint. Draw boats, trees, bugs, or whatever you like! Let the paint dry.

3 Place the painted rocks on newspaper. Coat them with spray sealer. Let them dry.

Rockimoes

1 Find 28 flat rectangular or oval rocks. Cover your work surface with newspaper.

2 Paint the rocks black. Let the paint dry.

3 Paint a line across each rock. Add dots. Follow the chart below.

4 Place the rockimoes on newspaper. Coat them with spray sealer. Let them dry.

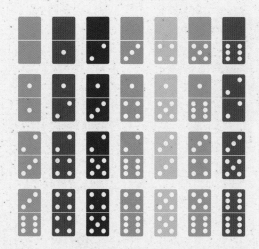

terra-cotta WIND CHIMES

Materials

newspaper
3 3½-inch (9 cm) terra-cotta pots
acrylic paint
paintbrushes
puffy paint
spray sealer
scissors
ruler
twine
large beads

1 Cover your work surface with newspaper. Paint the pots with a base color. Let them dry. Use puffy paint to decorate the pots. Let them dry. Coat them with spray sealer. Let them dry.

2 Cut a piece of twine about 36 inches (91 cm) long. Tie a double knot at one end. Put a bead on the twine. Push the bead to the knot.

3 Tie a knot about 2 inches (5 cm) above the bead. Put another bead on the twine.

4 Put the twine through the hole in the pot. Pull it until the bead hits the pot.

5 Tie a knot 2 inches (5 cm) from the bottom of the pot. Add a bead and the second pot. Add the third pot the same way.

6 Add three more beads above the third pot. Tie a knot between each bead. Tie a loop in the twine above the beads. Cut off the extra twine.

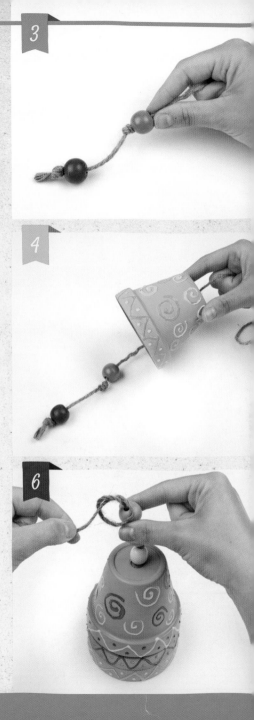

sun-printed
SCARF

Make a cool scarf on a sunny day!

Materials

newspaper
white cotton scarf
cardboard
scissors
plastic wrap
clear tape
fabric paint, 4 colors
5 plastic containers
measuring spoons
stir sticks
5 foam brushes
leaves
small stones
coarse sea salt
iron
ironing board

1 Cover your work surface with newspaper.

2 Cut a piece of cardboard the same size as the scarf. Cover the cardboard with plastic wrap. Tape the plastic wrap to the cardboard. Smooth the plastic flat on one side.

3 Tape the scarf over the plastic. Smooth out the scarf.

4 Prepare the paint. Put 2 tablespoons of each color in a separate plastic container. Add 4 tablespoons of water to each color. Stir the paint. Fill the fifth plastic container with water.

(continued on next page)

5 Paint the scarf with water until it is completely damp.

6 Paint the scarf with the first color. Use long, smooth strokes. Don't paint the whole scarf. Leave white space.

7 Paint part of the white space with another color. Use a different brush. Leave some white space.

TIP Cut shapes, animals, or other designs out of paper. Arrange them on the scarf instead of leaves.

8 Paint most of the white space with a third color. Use a different brush. Leave a little white space.

9 Paint any leftover white space with the fourth color.

10 Arrange the leaves on top. Work quickly. Press the leaves onto the fabric. Add stones to hold them down.

11 Sprinkle a handful of sea salt on the scarf. Place the scarf in the bright sun. Let it dry.

12 Remove the salt and plants. Rinse the scarf in warm water. Let it dry completely. Iron the scarf using the cotton setting for 2 to 3 minutes.

OUTDOOR tea lights

Candle holders to light your late-night picnic!

Materials

newspaper
mason jars and lids
Mod Podge
food coloring
toothpicks
clear tape
paper plates
gold paint
paintbrush
LED tea lights

1 Cover your work surface with newspaper.

2 Pour Mod Podge into a jar. Use enough to cover the inside of the jar.

3 Add a couple drops of food coloring. Mix the food coloring and Mod Podge together. Swirl the glue around to coat the inside of the jar.

4 Tape two toothpicks side by side on a paper plate. Set the jar upside down on top of the toothpicks.

5 Repeat steps 1 through 4 to coat more jars. Let the glue dry.

6 Paint the outside of the jars with gold paint. Decorate the lids too. Let the paint dry.

7 Put a tea light in each jar. Screw the lids on the jars.

no more pink FLAMINGOS!

Bring your inner artist outside!

Materials

newspaper
plastic yard flamingo
gold & blue plastic spray paint
blue painter's tape
acrylic paint
pencil
waterproof Gorilla Glue
googly eyes

1 Cover your work surface with newspaper. Take the legs off the flamingo.

2 Paint the beak gold. Use several light coats so the paint doesn't run. Let it dry completely after each coat.

3 Cover the beak with painter's tape. Start wrapping along the beak line. Cover the beak completely.

4 Paint the body of the bird blue. Let it dry completely. Add another coat if necessary and let it dry. Remove the painter's tape.

5 Use the eraser on a pencil to decorate the flamingo with colored polka dots.

6 Glue googly eyes to the head. Put the legs back on.

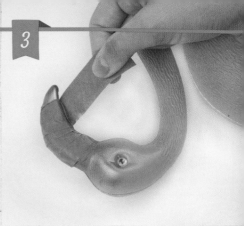

garden BLING

Make jewelry for
your garden!

Materials

ruler
plant stakes with hoops
permanent marker
large beads
black duct tape
drawer knob
waterproof Gorilla Glue

1   Measure 6 inches (15 cm) from the bottom of a stake. Mark the spot with a permanent marker.

2   Slide beads onto the stake. Stop adding beads when you get to the marker line.

3   Wrap black duct tape around the stake to hold the beads in place.

4   Glue the drawer knob to the top of the stake.

5   Repeat steps 1 through 4 to make more stakes. Put them in the garden.

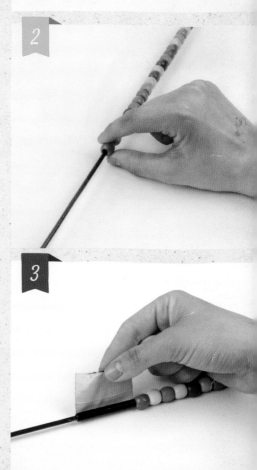

How Great Is the
GREAT OUTDOORS?

*D*id you enjoy creating nature art? Did any of the activities in this book inspire you to do more things in the great outdoors?

There is so much to love about being outside. These activities are just the beginning! Check out the other books in this series. You just might start spending more time outside than inside!

GLOSSARY

appropriately – in a manner that is suitable, fitting, or proper for a specific occasion.

balcony – a porch with railings outside an upper floor of a building.

flexible – easy to move or bend.

hospitality – generous and friendly treatment of guests so they feel welcome and comfortable.

muse – someone or something that an artist gets creative ideas from.

permission – when a person in charge says it's okay to do something.

supervision – the act of watching over or directing others.

variety – different types of one thing.

vitamin – a substance needed for good health, found naturally in plants and meats.

Websites

To learn more about Cool Great Outdoors, visit **booklinks.abdopublishing.com**. These links are routinely monitored and updated to provide the most current information available.

Index